Kidisms or Tales From a Teacher

Rita Kim Will

Dedication

I dedicate this book to all the children who went through my classroom. You were an inspiration for this book! Thank you for the laughter.

Acknowledgments

I want to acknowledge Trish, who was my partner in laughter.

About the Author

Rita Kim is a retired teacher. She spent 35+ years in the classroom working with children. She would always write down the funny things they did and said. Someday, she wanted to share these experiences so that people could see the lighter side of teaching.

Decisions

Teaching was not for me. I thought I wanted to be an interior designer. I started classes at the university for that major. They just didn't suit me. After a semester, I had changed my mind, and not knowing what to do next, I went undeclared my first year. What did I want to do? I did not want to teach. Why? I don't know. Everyone I knew wanted to be a teacher, so I decided I didn't want to be like everyone else. I never really felt like I was like everyone else.

I knew that I wanted to work with children because I have always loved all of my little cousins. I decided that I would like to run a daycare. I met with a school counselor who suggested I try a dual major in elementary education and early childhood. It sounded good to me.

The more I took classes and was out and about in the schools, I decided I loved the preparatory courses for teaching, being in the schools with children and maybe teaching wouldn't be so bad after all. The early childhood/developmental classes were also invaluable to me.

Teaching. Where you get to celebrate life. Where you get to help children, where you have many roles: a teacher, a mother, a nurse, a counselor, a mediator, and the list goes on.

Little did I know what was ahead for me. Teaching involves your whole self, your heart, your head, and so much more.

You get your diploma, apply for and get a job and there you are in a classroom with anywhere from 15-30 children. The rest is up to you. My first classroom teaching job was in an elementary first grade. I was so excited! I had written each child's name outside of my room on a big piece of chart paper, and then one of the second-grade teachers told me that I was making some of my letters wrong. I was upset because I had to do it all over again. Little did she know what that did to my self-esteem, something so small and insignificant in the scheme of things, but I was torn down because of that. I knew how children would feel just because of little comments made to them. The negative ones stick. And I wanted to remember that as I started my teaching career.

Some days were exhausting, and some children were exhausting. It was all part of being a teacher and loving this career path. I was there day after day because those children relied on me. I was the stabilizing part of their day, and they were the stabilizing part of mine.

I taught first, second, and then fourth grades. Fourth was my favorite. Those kids are so full of life, energy, excitement, creativity, friendships, figuring out life in their little selves, and being fourth graders. They can also be fidgety, testing the rules and the limits and making great strides in their learning.

Being a teacher is more than teaching kids to take a test. It is also not an 8-4 job with all weekends and holidays off.

I wrote this to make people laugh and realize that teaching for me has been rewarding in many ways. The children, co-workers, friends, and parents I have met will forever remain in my heart.

Any teacher has memories like this, and any teacher could write this book. These are my experiences, and I wanted to share them.

If you recognize yourself or your child in this book, I hope you will smile or laugh along with me. I can still visualize each moment I wrote about. They are precious memories for me, as are the students I taught.

Teacher Requirements

Or what they don't tell you

Have a sense of humor.

Be excited to see the kids every single day.

Realize that every day is a new day to begin again.

Be able to eat your lunch in 7 minutes or less, some days, or not at all.

Spend hours preparing your lesson plans, only to be able to change them at the last minute when something isn't working, something or someone interrupts the schedule, or there is an unplanned fire drill.

Know that glitter is never a good idea.

Have a strong bladder.

Realize you are never "all caught up", and you are okay with that.

You could have a second job as a weather forecaster because you know exactly when storms are moving in and when there is a full moon.

You know that smiling and nodding is sometimes the best way to go.

Have thick skin because children are so honest with your appearance and other things about you.

You are never bored.

Be funny and laugh at a child's joke, even when it isn't funny.

Listening to a child tell you ALL about their weekend from beginning to end.

Have a chocolate drawer and be willing to share it with all the people who know you have a chocolate drawer.

You cherish the calmness in the morning before the kids come in.

You also cherish the noise and smiles they bring with them.

You don't mind repeating yourself. You don't mind repeating yourself. You don't mind repeating yourself.

Know that a little nonsense is good, and sometimes a lot of nonsense is great.

You can listen to people say how lucky you are to be a teacher, working 8-4, with no weekends, holidays and summers off, and you just smile and nod.

You get a little upset when back-to-school supplies are advertised in June.

You believe in the right for every child to have the chance to learn.

You believe that every child has good qualities inside and that sometimes you need to work harder than the child to find these qualities and instill them in that child.

You need to reach the child before you can teach the child.

Testing is not first in your classroom; the child is.

Most importantly, you realize:

It is the little things that make the biggest difference.

Like an unexpected hug from a child.

Or a compliment from your co-worker.

Your coffee is still hot.

A parent writes you a nice note.

That AHA moment when a student "gets it".

Let's hear it for the teachers who keep children as children and still teach them the essentials they need to know to live a life as full and complete human beings.

Kidisms

or actual quotes from real kids

Ants work until they die. I wouldn't.

Stop being yourself.

I'm debating on whether or not to have my tonsils out.

What did your doctor say?

Oh, I haven't talked to a doctor. I'm just debating on it.

You are going to see a little bit of weirdness in me today.

This is a tough crowd.

That dinosaur is a vegetarian.

So, I guess this one is a meatatarian.

So, what does the word opportunity mean?

We have that opportunity room.

Trouble.

Are we going to discuss our goals and objections?

What does the teacher's lounge look like?

It's like a luxury in there.

Do you get free breakfast?

No, but you get food in the lounge. It's like a party.

I suffer every single day.

How do you spell…..?

It's my street name.

We have cannibals in our town.

S called me the p word.

Me–the P word?

Poopy pants.

When clouds rain, they let out their feelings.

P.E. is awesome. It works your abes.

Ms. Will, thank you for being my friend for years.

I didn't bring my planner today because I was looking for my soccer cleats because I have practice tonight. So yeah, I was out of my mind.

My sister said I was going to die old and alone with cats.

My throat is rusty.

What exactly is vodka?

You'll be all loopy, and you don't know what the heck you are doing.

I can't hear what I'm hearing.

How do you spell bw?

He can't understand the words she root. She root them in curfoose.

Every time I breathe in through my nose, air gets up in there.

Betty Ross made the first flag. I should have noon that.

What if you miss one of these? Would you get it wrong?

I can't think. My shoe fell off.

Do you put your name where it says date?

Something just creeped up in my brain.

Some perfumes alert my nose.

My computer went blank.
Try pressing the spacebar.
It works! I'm a genius!

Did you know that your tongue has a nose? Those are called taste buds.

Ms. W. is the meanest teacher I have ever had.
Why?
Because she makes you do your work.

I'm wearing Crocs. They are basically a new type of shoe.

Do you think that when we go home each day, the teachers say, "Thank God they are gone"?

The cursive e is like a backward 3.

Yeah, so the genius that thought that up, didn't have to think much.

Can you pull up your pants? Pull them up so they stay up. You really need bigger pants.

Why are your eyebrows so thin?

Do we have to color the sentences?

The 4 directions on the rumpus coze are north, south, east, and west.

I went to the sanitarium when I was little. You know, the one with all the fish.

How many pages are in a 200-page book?

A student wrote ovovue in a sentence. I asked him what that word was. He looked at me like I should know and said, "Of".

There was a sub the day before. One boy said to me:

B: I just can't act normal. Only when you are here, Ms. W.

Me: I understand that from my notes.

B: I know, right?!

Barney would strangle kids who did not know their ABCs.

So, say I'm a kid.

Conviction is when you get kicked out of your house.

It hurts when your problem doesn't work.

Students struggling with math

Me: What's 8 x 7?

S: 25?

Me: no

S: 36?

Me: no.

S: 7?

Me: No, you are just guessing.

S: exactly.

During journal writing in the morning, a student was singing a song.

Another one said: Stop doing that; you're embarrassing everyone.

We have a turtle at home. She had babies, so now we have 27. I mean, she had 98.

When a child wants you to notice something, but you don't, so they say:

Notice anything different about my elbows?

An assignment was to define tolerance.

One student wrote: willingness to be patient toward people whose opinions might be different from yours.

Give an example: My mom and dad drive me crazy.

I am terrible at this.

You don't have to be good at everything.

One boy was giving a spelling test to 3 of his peers.

I'll give you guys one more chance. If I hear a peep out of you I'm telling.

What does justice mean?
It's where you buy shirts.

I'm never going to pass my 12's. (Multiplication)
Well, not with that attitude.

See, I'm not crazy.
No one said you were.

Years ago when I was little...

After giving his biography presentation K said, I think I was gorgeous in the spotlight.

I'm silly on the inside. But I'm calm on the outside. I just have to get the laughs out.

Is Granadian a culture?

Do you have a cold lunch?

Yes.

Ok, that's a first.

I've had it a couple of times before.

Ok, that's a third.

When you have lobster, you have to pull the muscles out of it. That's sick.

M is pulling down her shirt and showing us her spots.

I'm playing soccer this summer.

Yeah, and I'm joining the circus.

L: (talking in Spanish)

M: What is she saying?

B: She just called you a butthead in Spanish.

Stop throwing a tude.

You are obviously in love.

Say a bad guy was coming.

A bad guy was coming.

A letter to a lady from the bank who came to the class:

Thank you for helping us to not waste a lot of money. The goal budgets I didn't get because I was kinda distrackted with someone.

I liked it when the green bean lady came. (soybean)

I had a cold, my throat was sore and I sounded awful.

You always sound like that.

A student was talking about the class next door.

How come they get computers and we don't? That is just unfair, outrageous, and unpleasant.

A boy was saying a word in Spanish, looked at me, and said, Do you know what that means?

Me: Yes, I know what that Spanish word means. I know what all the bad words are in Spanish. (I found out what they were after that, and he was saying a bad word)

We were doing potato stamping on sacks.

Ms. W calls this a mess. I say it's a masterpiece.

Two kids were talking about divorce.

It's like you are married. Then you break up.

There's a lot of paperwork.

Talking to a child about parent-teacher conferences:

Me: I haven't heard from your parents.

T: I haven't either.

We were getting books for a book report. I helped a boy find one for his.

Hmmmm, guess I'm going to have to read this.

Out of the blue to me-

You wear your age well.

Writing what they learned after visiting an art gallery

I learned nothing because it was so quiet. I learned, well, I didn't really learn anything.

To me: Did you put perfume on because you smell better than ever?

Me: Yes

You don't usually smell that way.

A student while turning in his late work: I'm just making your life easier.

When I returned after being gone:
We did all the wrong stuff yesterday.

Coming into the room on a Monday, some crayons were scattered all over the floor under a student's desk. After the group decided no one at their desks had done this, one student said:
Ms. W, We have a crime scene here.

You can be strict sometimes, but you are the best teacher I have had in years.

Watching mealworms: We've got a runner!
Let's name them. How do you tell if it's a boy or a girl?

We had gone on a field trip to the rodeo, which was at our fairgrounds and near our school. The cowboys always took us through the various rodeo events.

I had an autistic child that year, so he was walking with me. We were getting ready to go to the clowns.

He said that's a big NO on the clowns!

During the rodeo, we were to wear wristbands. He didn't want to. He took it off, gave it to me and said:

Let's just keep this between you and me. We won't tell the cowboys.

Walking back from the rodeo, a boy was walking beside me.

C: I like your phone.

Me: Thanks.

C: What kind did you have when you were my age?

Me: I thought for a moment and chuckled. Then I said, "We didn't have phones like this back when I was your age."

He just looked at me and never said another word!

Somehow, in a small reading group, we got on the subject of strokes. One of the girl's uncles had just had one. We discussed that and then went on to heart attacks. They thought you could put steel into a heart to make it work better.

Then, a boy told me he had a heart attack the week before.

Hmmmmmm

Overheard in the library while we were checking out books:

T: Are you looking for shark books to impress girls?

B: No, I want to see how you get bitten by sharks.

T: laughing.

B: If you would stop laughing at me. I would appreciate it.

T: I'm not laughing.

B: Then what is that chuckle about?

I have this feeling I just want to create something.

Write a sentence using "to shop for". My mom went to shop for a new dad.

Writing a thank you to our college girl. We had two students, a boy and a girl, from the college for a semester. (Ms. B and Mr. P)

Dear Ms. B,

Thank you for being a nice person. You are very pretty. You will have 25 guys after you. My advice is not to date Mr. P at all.

A note from one girl to another:

L: I think a boy is cute. His name is J.

K: I think he is cute too, but you don't stand a chance with him. Get a life.

Some kids left for a small reading group. That teacher was showing the girls her nails.

One of the boys said: Is this some kind of a nail salon place? Because this is NOT what I paid for.

You know–men-type people.

This paint feels drier than a kangaroo. I don't even know if a kangaroo is dry.

How do you even make infinity a number when you write it?

A child in my class got into a character club, a club where you are a student who always follows the rules. He said: I didn't see that coming.

If you adore something, it means you really love it no matter what.

Saying goodbye on the last day of school is going to leave a sunburn in my heart because you make my day with a little tiny smile.

Things I have said to kids

Who brought the snake in their backpack?

Any toys you bring this year will be taken. You can buy them back at my garage sale next summer.

I can't give out any more gum this year at the end of the day. Mr. H (the principal) stepped in some outside. I don't think it was his first time.

Who smells like they dumped a bottle of cologne on themselves? Every child pointed to the culprit. Will you take it home, or should I call your mom?

It is just raining outside. (Everyone got up and ran to the window) Go back to your seats unless you have never seen rain before.

No, I don't have extra shoes in my desk drawer, like your teacher from last year did. But that is a good idea!

Chips are not a healthy snack.

Ask someone who was listening the first time I gave the directions.

I did not say we would get an extra recess. Who heard me say that? (All hands go up)

Following are some notes written to discuss at a class meeting. They could write them on a paper taped to a bulletin board before our class meeting. You could not write anyone's name unless you had their permission. So, they had to put "someone." The following is just for ONE class meeting!

Someone is gossiping about something in music.

Someone keeps blaming J for no reason.

In Music 2 girls where mad at me because I was in the wrong spot, and they were in chariucter club.

Someone was saying in your face and I told you so. Even though I was right.

Someone was lesening to my cdonforsathen and buting in on privet confersaythens.

Someone isputing there stuff on my desk.

Someone is talking about dating.

Someone is reading the agenda to see if they are on here.

Someone tried to punch me.

People are saying do I need to call the wambulance.

I have a problem people are talking about.

People are talking about me at a table in the lunch room behind me.

Finally a positive one:

I can show the class how to make paper cranes.

And on and on. These are very important in the life of a 4th grader. We tried to solve them each week, and then new ones popped up—the next week. Lots of times, when we got to the problem, the student would say, I forgot. Or it's solved.

A lot of students put up ideas, too.

Before the meetings started, we went around the room and had to say something nice about someone, something, or to someone.

It was a great time to get things out in the open to solve problems and also get ideas!

Notes Written to me (unedited):

I like the way you always incourage kids.

You are a grat techer and I like your pants.

I love your hair it is very pretty and i like the color to. I like you as ur techer.

I like your shouse.

I like how you are nice.

Your the best teacher I've had sence 2nd grade.

I like how you help me in math and I like how you let us get candy if we get the anser right and i like you can we have an extra recess.

You are so nice I love your great ideas I love to come to school because you are here you make my day.

I promise I will be god the rest of the year. You are vevey vevey party.

Your kids are lucky to have you forever as a mother. You are an amazing reader for a teacher.

I liked when you taught math because you knew all the answers.

I want you to be my teacher for another 6 years, but then I'd get kinda tired of you. I am thankful for you because you help people accomplish the world.

Seeing you was the most exiting day of my life.

I hope you will have a wonderful weekend. I know we will have a wonderful school year. Everybody had a wonderful week, well that's what I heard.

I want to go back in time to start school all over. Then I would have a very good year all over again. But I know that won't happen so I should not cross my fingers.

Written in a journal:

Today I feel great because you are here today. I hope you stop getting sick. (I was gone one day)

I am ready to get some learning today and I am happy to do it.

And I HAVE to put this in:

There are a bunch of wonderful things about you: you're smart, fun, funny, beautiful, wonderful, exciting, thoughtful, great, beyond amazing, and especially a good teacher.

This is also a shout-out to all teachers!

Funny things in my classroom

Or Funny-isms in the classroom

Journal starter today: What is the funniest thing that has happened this year?

The class was asking about what to write. I said, "Oh, there have been a lot of funny things." Then, I couldn't honestly come up with one at that moment.

One of the boys said, "I know, it was when Ms. W. stood on her head the other day."

Another girl said, "That wasn't funny. That was talent."

I did that because we had finished all of our testing, and I told them I would do it when we were done. It was impressive, I know, although another boy could do it too, and if we had timed the both of us, he would have won.

We didn't time it. I didn't want to be outdone by a fourth grader.

It was the end of the year, fun times. It was all during math. We could have been learning about vertical lines. Or not. We could have just been having fun. Is there a test for that? I hope not.

***

Here are some ideas about friends the class wrote in their journals:

You can never judge a person until you know them.

You can't change a person.

People don't always change when they grow up. Pick the right friends.

Your truer friends will not ditch you.

I've learned I can make more friends by changing my attitude.

My friends pick me up when I fall down.

It doesn't matter what others think of you, whatever you think of yourself, that's what you are.

*****

A fourth grader's perspective: Who is Santa Claus?

A nice, jolly old elf that not only gives toys but also love to everyone on earth.

Do you believe in Santa Claus? Explain.

Yes, because he gives toys to all of the kids and my dad said he worked with Santa. He looked like he did. So I believe him.

Have you always felt this way about Santa Claus?

Yes, for ten years, of course, I believe in Santa.

Will you always feel the way you do?

Yes, Santa's only important job is loving each boy and girl and that's why I believe.

*****

During small group reading, we were all on a child-friendly site. Or so I thought. I told them to look up Native Americans. They had some questions to answer. Student A comes up to me and says B is typing inappropriate words. B denies it vehemently and says A typed it in. So I look at the history, and it says: Search for Penis.

Luckily, we were on a safe website, so nothing came up.

A said B did it. B said A did it. Both were denying it. So I asked C, and she said she was in the bathroom and didn't see anything.

I decided to walk around the room more.

***

One day, in math, I had the kids work with a partner to decide whether our "penguin" friend in the book had completed a problem correctly or incorrectly. (He was always wrong.)

After a while, the kids decided he was right because they had worked out the problem.

I said, "No, you are all wrong." (That's probably not the best way to word it, but it was a Monday.) One of the kids said, "You are smiling, so we are right."

Another one said: She is always smiling, even when she drinks her coffee in the mornings.

***

I got my hair colored. When I got to school the next day, the class just stared and no one said anything. In the afternoon, during math (which we always did in a small group in the back of the room on the floor first.)

One child finally said: What did you do to your hair?

I said: I colored it.

Another child said:: Are you wearing eye shadow?

I said: Yes.

He then said: Look, everyone, Ms. W. is wearing purple eyeshadow.

It's ok, girls can do that.

The moral of that story: Anything is better than doing division. And I was still thought of as a girl.

***

Another time, I had my hair cut and colored. It was quite different. Some comments I got were:

What did you do to your hair?

Why did you do that?

Did you do something to your hair? It's kind of red.

I said: No, it's cocoa.

Well, I see red.

I like it, but I will need to get used to it.

***

I loved that children noticed everything. Some days, anyway.

Are you tired today?

Me: No, why?

You look really tired.

Well, thanks.

***

Two more days were left of the school year. Some quotes from me:

Yes, this still counts for a grade.

I can take away your recess, you know.

Yes, I'm sure I've had enough coffee. Why would you ask?

It's still up to me whether you go on to that next grade.

Is anyone listening to me? Then what did I just say?

We are now on a zero talking time. Zero means no talking, none at all. No, you can't whisper because that is still talking.

Yes, technically it is.

Because I said so, that's why.

Raise your right hand if you are listening to me. Your right one.

No, the other right.

***

One day in math, I had a few extra minutes and decided to teach the class about matter and mass (as per the teacher's edition.)

We drew an elephant, cat, and ant on our whiteboards. I started giving them examples. They all looked at me like I was nuts.

One girl said: I don't get this at all.

Then a boy in the class said: Is this another one of your April fool's jokes?

Maybe if I had started with an elephant, a cat, and an ant walked into a bar . . .

***

Conversations while observing our mealworms.

Things I said:

No, we are not eating the mealworms. I don't care that you ate them in second grade; we still aren't eating them.

Yes, I understand that your aunt eats them.

Don't blow on the wheat germ.

Stop putting the mealworms on her shirt.

No, they don't turn into butterflies.

They are not our class pets. No one is taking them home.

***

I took advantage of the only nice day in a week and took the solar panels outside to try and get the motors to run. The panels were new and wrapped in bubble wrap.

How many ways can you say stop popping the bubble wrap? Or just–Let it go!

Popping bubble wrap could be our next experiment because we were so good at it.

***

One class was so talkative that I told them they would go to lunch when they were quiet. They were still talking, so I got out my lunch and started eating and reading a book. They were quiet almost immediately, and I let them sit for a couple of minutes and then said, "Oh, you decided to quiet down? I was just eating my lunch. It's my time now." I let them go, and getting them quiet the next day was easier.

***

A student who had been in some trouble off and on during the year asked to use the phone on the wall by the secretary's desk after school. He wanted to call home to see if he was to walk home or if someone was picking him up. He said he had forgotten. A little while later, a phone call came from a pizza place asking if the student had ordered a pizza. He had given his real name and wanted it delivered to the school!

The principal called the student into his office the next day and asked him if he had ordered a pizza. He admitted it, and the principal told him that he and his wife enjoyed it but that he still owed for the pizza! He had him do some work around the school to pay for it.

***

I liked to call kids up to the floor to sit and listen to me read stories. Once on the first day of school, I was reading, and someone said, "Look a snake!" A garter snake crawled among the kids, and one boy grabbed it and said: I got it! He got to take it outside. No idea where it came from. The kids asked if I was afraid of snakes, and I lied and said no.

***

Another snake story is when someone brought one in their backpack. In the morning, the kids ratted him out. He was refusing to admit it. I called him up to my desk, and I calmly said, go out to your backpack, take the snake out, and take him outside. He did.

***

My teaching partner and I were talking in the hall when the kids had gone to specials. Here came a good-sized garter snake. We both ran into our rooms, got on our desks, and yelled at each other to go get it. We didn't. We yelled down the hall to see if the custodian was around. He wasn't. Mr. B. a 6th grade teacher, finally heard us, came down, and scooped up the snake. He also gave us a look like, "really"?

***

There were times when nothing would work except for writing the directions on the overhead. One group was so talkative that my co-worker and I simply wrote STOP TALKING. And sat down until they did. We are still sitting.

***

We had a one-story school. Whenever we had to use the restroom, my co-teacher next door and I would stand outside each other's classrooms and say, "I need to go downstairs." We would watch each other's classes. This confused the kids, and I think they thought we had a hidden basement somewhere. They never asked, so we never told them.

***

Our fifth-grade teacher was walking down our hallway talking to us, turned the corner to her room, and ran smack dab right into a cupboard. We were laughing so hard that it took a while to regain our composure and make sure she was alright. We taped a big Caution sign on it, then. (She was alright)

***

We were in our classes one day early in the school year, and the alarm went off, so we all did what we were supposed to and went outside. The bell rang, we came back in and the principal said we did a good job of getting out of the building quickly and quietly. After school, he called a short meeting.

He said, "Good job on the drill, getting out of the building quickly and quietly. There is a small problem. That was a tornado drill.

(In our defense, well, we really don't have an excuse, but we had a good laugh) It wasn't tornado season, and so . . . We will stick with that. (And a child had pulled it on purpose)

***

I only lost one parent on a field trip. And her child. Twice. I had given directions to meet at a certain spot in 30 minutes. We had 48 kids and about 24 parents. Each parent was in charge of their own child and maybe 2-3 more. We were at a museum and headed for an art gallery. At the art gallery, we were to silence our phones and leave all our backpacks downstairs. So I did. The student and his mother came out of the museum wondering where we were. She did not speak English, so she called the school and the interpreter called me, but my phone was in my backpack!

Luckily, they got a hold of the other teacher, and she came and said," Do you know where J and his mother are?"

I said, "They are here somewhere."

She said, "No, he and his mother are at the museum."

I went to get them and told her how sorry I was, and I also asked J what the directions were. He didn't know because listening was a weakness of his.

His mother blamed him for never listening, and we had a good laugh. Really it was my fault. Then on the way to the stadium for a tour, they got lost again!

A parent said, "I will go get them."

I have never lived that one down.

Remember the time you lost a child and his parent on a field trip? It's always funny when it's not you.

***

I assigned Native American dioramas for the kids to do at home. I knew they would have parent help and that was ok, as long as it was a family effort.

S: My dad stayed home from work today.

Me: Oh no, is he sick?

S: No, he is working on my diorama.

***

Some days, you feel like you are talking to a brick wall because it feels as if no one is listening. When ordering for the next year, the other teacher and I got a brick wall border, put it between our two rooms on the wall vertically, and frequently, one of us would go out there and just lean our head on it. Brick wall moments.

***

We also had so many squirrel moments; if you are a teacher, you know what that is. You are talking, or a child is talking to you, and you get distracted and then can't remember what you are talking about. You can also be teaching, and a random thought comes into your head, so you divert to that! Kids do it all the time.

You ask a question about something, say geography, a hand goes up, and you call on them.

They say: We got a new dog on Saturday.

Squirrel moment.

***

We would "surround" kids at times. This involved just having two teachers talking with one child. Most of it was positive, and we took turns telling the child what he/she was good at. We also asked them how they liked school and what they didn't like. We told them one thing they could work on. They loved this.

***

On the other side, if something had happened on the playground and we kind of had an idea of what had gone on, we would surround a child and say, "We already know what happened, so we would like to hear your side of this.'

Most of the time, we didn't know. Only once did a child refuse to own up.

Sometimes, when doing this, one of us would get the giggles so much that we could hardly stand there. And then would say, "Oh, I just thought of something funny."

***

One of my girls came to school one day with makeup on. (Obvious makeup) I commented on it.

Me: I noticed you are wearing makeup today. Did your mom help you put that on?

K: No, I did it myself.

Me: Did your mom see it before you left?

K: Yes.

Me: So if I call her and ask her about it will she say she saw you or do you want to go wash it off?

K: I'll go wash it off.

***

I got a note from one of the girls when I got back from being gone:

We got a lot of work done, and we got double points yesterday. But fifth grade had to trade subs with us because they were so noisy. They had to call a minister from downtown.

***

A student's spelling homework was turned in on a "Happy Birthday" napkin. They didn't have any paper and he figured out how to get it done.

***

Another student's parent wrote me a note about their cat who chewed up the corner of the homework sheet. They did it anyway the best they could and sent it in with the corner chewed off!

***

My dog ate the homework–or actually my dog chewed up 2 books! The parents had gotten a new puppy and he chewed up 2 of my personal books I had loaned to their son! They offered to replace them, but hey, things happen.

***

In science, one day we were learning about carnivores, herbivores and omnivores. The conversation took a turn to "cannibals who eat people, and they are naked." The next child said we had cannibals in our city.

I said: No, we don't have cannibals here in our city.

Then, a "squirrel moment" happened, and the conversation turned to steak. I said I didn't like steak.

K: My mom makes really good steak.

Me: I'm sure she does, but I still don't like steak.

K: I have never known ANYONE who doesn't like steak.

And then, science was over. Where is my chocolate?

***

We were beginning a new writing activity. It was about a memory. I always modeled one first and I was typing so they could see my story on the screen. It was about a trip to Florida that I went on with my son. I was a 7th and 8th grade sponsor.

I typed: We got to the airport and were stopped by security. My son's backpack had beeped and they wouldn't let us through until the people in security had checked it. We had to wait a while because they had to call someone to come look at it.

We were on our way to: and this is where they all yelled—JAIL?

Um, no, actually, Orlando.

***

We were on the bus coming home from our annual field trip to Lincoln. One student had been particularly challenging at certain times of the trip. So, he was my partner on the trip. He sat ahead of me on the bus and fell asleep for about an hour. It was an hour-and-a-half trip. Then he woke up.

A: Wow, was I asleep for a while?

Me: Yes, about an hour. The quietest part of my day.

A: Really? Cool.

I did enjoy the laughter of the children on the way home. It was enlightening. The kind of laughter that comes from their gut and makes you want to laugh along with them. It lasted the whole bus ride home.

Teaching lives, touching lives

The way teachers affect children's lives is ongoing. You may be someone who made "that difference" and never know it. You may be someone they will always remember. You just know you did your best for them. And sometimes you find out things years later.

A former student came up to me and said I am going to college to become a teacher. You inspired me.

A mother at a local grocery store was checking me out. I had her son years before when I taught 1st grade. She said, "I never thanked you for figuring out my son could not read, and you are the reason he is successful today." (He was memorizing everything, and I got him help)

It is special when, as a 4th grade teacher, you get invited to graduation parties. One boy I had in my class was having his party, and his mom asked which teachers to invite. He said he just wanted his favorite one, me.

The end

Or–the beginning

It's all in your outlook

You have bonded with those children in your classroom the minute they walk in the first day, and it grows throughout the year. You know they were infinitely more significant than the subject matter you were teaching. They have become your family, and you have to let them go and move on to the next experience in their lives. It is tough saying goodbye. Knowing you have done all you can to touch each life can be a relief, a good one.

The notes the students write to you are a precious part of why you teach.

Every year, you are the best teacher they have ever had. And you know they say it every year to every teacher, but somehow, it reaches your heart because they truly mean it.

I KNOW I MADE A DIFFERENCE.

A teacher walked into my room and couldn't see me. She said, "What did you do, eat your teacher?"

J, "Yes, we ate our way to her heart."